PULSE

Peter Knight

Acknowledgements

In memory of my immigrant ancestors:

Richard Troy Knight, born 1830, St Pancras, London, England; music hall performer & entrepreneur;

died 1912, Lidcombe, New South Wales

His wife Mary Knight [nee Cookson], born 1831, Burslem, Staffordshire, England; died 1891,

Collingwood, Victoria

James Frederick Meredith, born 1824, Knighton/Trefyclawdd, Radnorshire/Powys, Wales; ship's

purser; died 1896, Blackwood, Victoria

His wife Margaret Priscilla Meredith [nee Robertson] born 1831, Dundee, Scotland; died 1923,

North Trentham, Victoria

PULSE
ISBN: 978-1-76109-721-8
Copyright © text Peter Knight 2026
Cover image: by Graham Davidson

First published 2026 by
GINNINDERRA PRESS
PO Box 2 Bentleigh 3204
ginninderrapress.com.au

Contents

Spin

    bring 'em out   7
    spinning top, can't stop   9
    Heartless: a sacrifice   11
    the art of a diver   13
    'a quick & peaceful end'   15
    If not pain…   18
    when two   20
    blood red arose   21

Spring

    3 degrees of tree   25
    planted   28
    terminal   30
    Boggart Hole Clough   31
    into the trees (ENORMITY)   35
    Sprung   37
    flight of the better-fly   39

Consumption

    See, hear…act   43
    consumption   44
    Ablaze!   46
    Oh, see…   47
    Big Top Emotion   49
    Too Big   51
    it's little niggling things   56

Notice Me
- the kiss — 59
- smoking desire on Psych Ward 2B — 61
- Notice me (Assurance) — 64
- your dying, your memory — 67
- really & imaginable — 71
- Imacello — 73
- footsteps, dance floor — 75

About the Author — 77

Spin

bring 'em out

Bring out your dead,
drag out your bloodied and bled,
don't hide your festering shame,
today is cast away day.

Fling out that which is rotten,
don't stomach the smell
of soured flesh and spirit,
be moved by my call
to bring out your dead.

Bring out your wounded
that they may be healed.
Root out your corruption,
sling it with your greed.

Banish your traumas
and drugged notions,
throw up your untruths,
don't remain tangled in delusion,
believe, you can do.

Dump your crippled
and paralysing ways,
rid yourself of that morass,
no longer worship idols,
their removal
will gift you peace.

Now raise your head and look anew
at the Earth, the sun and the moon,
the planets, stars and galaxies
for what they are,
solid indications
of the heavenly
in your universe,
bring them into view.

spinning top, can't stop

Seated, hand in hand
snugly held, we are set off
on our pleasure ride.

Quickly our handhold
tightens to a clench
as we chug along
the upward slope
to our first roller coaster drop.
Then furious downhill displacement,
our senses spinning as we go,
caught in a chilling ride,
veering abruptly at corners,
forced across our seats.
With each overwhelming wrench,
we are moved, being tested of our resolve.

Sickening, (I think of jumping off),
my centre is displaced,
overwhelmed by velocities
that are too sharp, too sudden,
too insistent, for me to overcome.

I am driven beyond my limits i cry,
and am looking to be separated,
I from you.
I'm heard. Others stop.
Passers-by stand-look-listen,
(what drives such a wobbly decline?)

Our union is now unsprung,
(a relief that it's done!)
our ride run,
me vomiting up and forcing out
this passing fare, my attraction to you.

When stopped,
I am so swayed in my stride
that I topple onto my side
and sprawl and crawl
to recover my gait.
I'm staggering back
toward a life without as much spin,
steadier, a much spun top,
but no better balanced
for losing you.

Heartless: a sacrifice

1. I do not want to slay you,
but I do want to carve out
the source of the pound
of your bleating, beating heart.
I don't want to butcher you,
I just want to excise that beat
for which purpose I wield my knife.

I will cut away your flesh,
rupturing your arteries and veins,
grasping your vital part so exposed,
and amid a flood of blood,
tug your heart from its strings.

2. I don't want to forecast
your heart's weathers anymore.
my feeling for you is now outrage.
My impulse to mutilate you
may seem resistible,
yet I wish to gut you,
lift your pulsing organ into the air,
holding it to the light to denigrate.

3. Your excavated heart thumps
even when held high by me,
as in a pagan sacrifice,
cupped in my hands,
above its accustomed surrounds.

I let go my awe of you
and slip your organ
into a stainless steel tray.
Your heartless piece of meat,
is still beating, entreating me,
destined for disposal,
preferably by slow burning in Hell.

the art of a diver

To find you, I plunge, my hands pushing aside sea,
to put that above behind me, to look ahead, to being free.
The body of my desire propels my legs to thrash,
taking the labouring bulk of a diver into still deeper chill.

I'm some short distance down and already above my head
sits a crushing volume of water,
murky doubts surface with pending.
Sunlight, penetrating, dissolves to dim haze
as I warily descend.

Still, I am attracted, taken by the lure of the desired,
wanting to explore, to swim toward a new life,
not sure what to expect, but knowing what I must do
to realise my wish to share breath with you.

Sound slurs with my deepening.
Explosive bursts of my air ascending
in boisterous globules become faint to me.
The tiniest bubbles that escape into my blood
frolic within my head.
They liberate imaginings as they spread,
a chorus sings that previously unheard by me.

I search for you,
hoping to see clearly beyond my mask's rim,
past the condensation that films my vision.
To catch you, I will follow your bait,
bite on your hook.

I'm immersed
in my dream of our enduring embrace,
your touch, your arms, your face;
your face pressed into my glass.
I'm straining to see you,
my sight is failing, I'm feeling faint,
a strange bliss overcoming me…

'a quick & peaceful end'

(An unsworn deposition for a coroner inquiring into the disappearance of an American couple while scuba diving from a tourist dive boat at a Coral Sea reef.)

1. My energy is utterly depleted
from the ordeal of my struggle
from reef to shore.
A quick and peaceful end
is what I wished,
not to be swept into mangrove
and not be able to push away.

I'm burnt on my face and head,
from my exposure to the sun.
My skin is overtaken
by a raw red rash
inflamed by saltwater.

A big-beaked black bird
waits at the mangrove shore
maybe to peck at my eyes.
Trapped and exhausted,
there is little I can do
to deter its intent.
Maybe it will fly away.

2\. She is not with me now.
I had to push her away
after supporting her body
for a long while.
She drifted from my view.
Things may have since happened
to her that I don't want to know.

Did she suspect
that I delayed our ascent
from the sea floor to the dive-boat
for my want of wishing to go back?
She didn't say.
I didn't expect that we would be
so soon out of view of the boat,
abandoned to the seas,
likely to be sought out
to be savaged by sharks.

3. I relive the horror of these darkening seas,
thru crippling scenes of imagined shark frenzy,
while my fatigue-wrenched body, cramping,
presses its overwhelming plea for rest.

The black bird, since flown away, now returns,
its beak sharp and pointed. It approaches.
It intends to jab at my eyes at its leisure.

I wished for a quick and peaceful end
to remove me from my living misery,
to escape life with minimal trauma,
not anticipating a strange and savage ending
while tangled in the mangrove shore
of a savage and strange land.

If not pain...

1. If not for pain,
I could bear the stings inflicted by slings shot
and the impact of shafts of cutting misfortune
that mark me.

If not for pain,
I could spring free from the vice grip
of bodily ache inherited from crippling years
that hold me back from what I could do.

If not for pain,
I could withstand daily assault
on my brain and senses with some equanimity.

If not for the thought of pain,
I could keep secrets sought to be exposed by torture
(blood, run and bone and tendon stretched) to myself.

And if not for pain,
I could accept the Earth and all in it,
although all is not well in the world.

2. If not for pain, I could rise above
the scourging of my back,
the press of thorns into my head,
the hammering of nails into my flesh,
my knees smashed,
a spear thrust into my flank.
I am stripped naked.

I could endure this
for humanity, past, present and to be,
to absolve them from their misdeeds,
that they may be forgiven
and without pain.

3. If not for…
I may speak with you,
anticipating that you may want
to share yourself with me,
be mine as I would be yours.

when two

We are storm-powered,
moved by ice-rain blasts,
shifted by crosswinds,
riding great oceanic swells.

And when we two,
like looming icebergs
in headlong rush meet,
our flanks crash and grind,
until we crack and splinter,
thrust by the surge
by which we are driven.

We are bound as ice to ice,
until the Atlantic strength
of the waves we brave
overwhelms us
and our coupling is spent.

Fragments of foam
being blown and scattered,
we are left to the debris of our encounter,
bobbing on the crazy peaks and troughs
of our separation.

And although still in sight
of one another,
we fathom that we drift alone,
on sullen seas, again.

blood red arose

a red rose may radiate sorrow,
its thorns drawing brilliant dark blood
from its serpentine veins
that pulse within a dark mass below.

its blush buds burst
into claret crowns
wrapped in satin folds,
spiralled, stunning,
to acclaim exposed

and to strange surrounds,
the changing moods of winds,
the sharp penetration of light,
the encroaching advance of decline,
now unveiled.

a red rose beholds this all
and pales and withers
and weeps.

Spring

3 degrees of tree

1. Not too far away
a tree thunders to the ground
forcing out a blast of air and fume and smoke.
Having been felled
by hands directing a chainsaw's frenzy,
it's stripped naked to a log,
bound with chains, and trucked away,
leaving its severed limbs
and mangled crown of leaves.

Its stump, a dwarfed amputee,
oozes resin that sets to seal a scar,
a mark of the initial ferocity required
for a giant tree to be reduced
to pulp and chip.

2. Nearby, trees quietly harden.
Their trunks and limbs will shed bark
– in anticipation of the same end?
They slowly strip down
to spectres of trees
amid those living.
Ghostly gums hold out
their limbs and branches
the same as others,
but they no longer sway,
whichever way the wind.

These living, although exposed,
are for now reprieved
from the tree-fellers' lust for wood,
their continuing apprehension
marked by the withering of their flesh.

3. Nearer still, beneath canopies,
surviving others' toppling,
young thatches rise and thicken as undergrowth,
thriving with the opened-up penetration of light
thru space where others once stood.

And although lying within the probable future path
of the fall of more of the giant of their kind,
they trust that their prospects for growth
will not be crushed by a calamitous fall.

planted

While i stand tall, i lie
in wait and gather what I can,
sunlight and water.
At times i collect too little
or too much or too late.
Or that which i catch escapes,
grounded and exposed, as i am,
by my stationary fate.

My trunk braces
my upward extensions
that support my leaf-clad extremities.
Below me, a network of roots and fibres
spreads thru the dirt seeking sustenance
and anchors me against disturbance.

Fixed, i cannot uproot to save myself
from imminent harm or death,
although i bend whenever I can.
With greater force
i can be broken
or terminally displaced,
being the inherent risk
of my commitment to just one place.

When light penetrates leaves
and rain runs down,
and nourishment is drawn
from beneath,
all three meet and fuse
to spark a green current
sufficient to maintain my claim
to stand longer in this place,
and, with some effort,
for me to push out
some modest indicator
of budding growth.

terminal

1. When does a plant die?
Upon its first observed wilt
or browning of tips on its leaves?
The flow of its sap slowed inside?
The hardening of veins within its thinning skin?
Its increased labor to maintain a semblance of green?

Is it when trodden upon or trampled aside?
Or, when left to linger, become languid
and bloom shedding?
Is it when seen sparse-leaved and flagging?
Or browning to brittle, hollowed wood?
Or collapsing from rot, resistance crushed?

2. When do you and I die?
How long the struggle before
with life's melancholic ache?
The inevitable curtailment of sensibilities?
Functioning barely sufficient to suggest extant life?
Before irreversible black overwhelms you?

Is there any exactitude as to the onset
of life's irrevocable demise?
Do we accept death when it first presents?
Steadily shedding our leaves?
When death has already made its mark
and passed on?

Boggart Hole Clough

(Boggart Hole Clough is an old nature reserve in suburban Greater Manchester. A boggart is a supernatural creature, goblin-like, in Lancashire folklore. A clough is a gorge or narrow ravine.)

There are more things
stirring in hedge and copse
than eyes can see,
yet nothing escapes me.

Mischief fomented,
derision crowed,
the muffling of sorrow,
the gasping for help.
For me there is no recourse,
no choice but to be host to these.

1. I'm draped with folds,
wrapped about with trees,
clay underfoot, debris and sodden peat,
carved with hurrying streams,
flanked by high embankments,
steep-sided wooded risings,
home to dank hollows,
in which chill gathers at night.

Beneath this,
there is a welling
that may choke me upon further telling.
An undermining, grinding presence below,
from where others' eyes are open,
an imminence unseen under daylit skies,
that awaits the darkening,
cover, disguise.

2. Darkfall,
when evening glows electric,
when, under filament, long shadows flit,
silence sits unspoken,
broken by the sounds of scuffling,
of someone's struggles.
I am perturbed.

I have no voice
with which to challenge
these roused night fiends
emerging from underground
with harm intending,
their fists clenching
and devilment set in their eyes.
their ancient mischief,
boiling again on the hob,
brews with renewed vigour.
They invoke spirits of the dead
to join the living of their kind
in their temporary abode.

I cannot be other
than witness to their offence,
their breaking my bushes
and picket fences
to fuel their fires' flames,
with which to keep away
their seasonal antagonists
settled upon this winter's night.
Nothing, as such, escapes me.

3. Wearied,
I must keep alert
amid damp, mist
and freezing fog,
thru to the first blink
of the eye of day,
upon which they
and their co-conspirators retreat,
leaving me to want to be
as iI was once
but can no more.
Aye, there's the rub.

into the trees (ENORMITY)

1. for what appeared
from a distance
to be a wooden invitation,
still we did not turn away,
we had come so far.

we approach a shredded forest,
a few trees standing upright,
with foliage stripped, trunks bared,
a sight evidencing
a most unnatural event.

we step into these trees,
past glazed trunks and shattered stumps.
The trees that withstood
an apparent blast are not rejuvenating,
neutered by the persisting afterglow
of a radioactive burst that flashed,
maybe momentarily, through their ranks.

we reach to touch some timber,
our fingers running tentatively
upon glazed surfaces.
We immediately withdraw
our careless hands,
regretting experiencing
the ferocious transfer of heat
from irradiated timber to our flesh.

2. we hear falling sounds, abrupt,
as more branches are shed.
Feeling contaminated,
we mean to flee this dying plantation,
anxious to put its dirty transmission behind us.

We need not dwell long
upon the remnants
of such violence
to appreciate the ENORMITY
of that wrought,
and of that which may yet come.
We fast retreat from our revelation.
We must run to deliver its message
while we can.

Sprung

It can no longer be contained.
It has burst its restraining bubble
with thrusts that stab a warning
of a harsher regime to come.

Once sunk within winter's fold,
grey cloud cotton-woolled,
the sun now emerges
like a white boil erupting
upon the face
of a clearing sky.

Looking up toward the sun,
my eyes fix for a moment,
then in necessary deference
turn away,
pained by its fierce pulse of bright light,
even at this, its season of filtered shine.

Chill winds scour our faces,
cold bluster blows
icy sharp once again.
Winter weary plants lie wary,
forewarned by the sun's sudden strike,
touched by its untimely reach.
Its upcoming dominance
cannot be suppressed.

These blear months past
imposed a cold endurance upon us.
Now, this warmth lately sprung
has me sweltering in my winter weight.

flight of the better-fly

1. i set off into the air on gossamer thin wings.
I am earth-bred, lately full grown, let loose into the sky.
My recent emergence sees me seek out fascinators,
and to alight to indulge to my satisfaction for a first time.

Near-to-ground, i easily rise and dip,
hedge-hopping shaggy heads of grass
and eruptions of weeds of seasonal opportunity.
I'm seeking ground where strange attractors sway.
With long necks and heads of coloured plume,
they move to the nudge of each breeze
that wafts.

2. i navigate, ultra-light, love-lifted,
bouncing off pockets of dense air,
aero-droning in for a landing.
On my approach to a strange attractor
another tempts me
from that course i seek to take.

i am abruptly drawn to shift my attention
to yet another attractor,
more arresting in its display,
more alluring, its scent
enticing me, a befuddled inebriate,
flying to its hidden liquor cabinet.

3. While i journey,
i may be spied by the unseen in the sky,
by eyes in heads, beaks and claws appended,
vigilant watchers who scan below for prey.
I hover about, hopefully on the sly,
not lingering about my love objects too long.
Cause and its effect may come into play
and catch me unawares one nightmare day.

4. My wings have become weighted,
stiffening and brittled with the demands
of my frenetic love-flights.
I'm slowed, hoping not to be overtaken,
as I near my next perfumed delight.
With a darting thrust, a small, agile bird
with large predator appetite,
dives and catches me in flight.

I'm mistaken for a moth in all likelihood,
snatched, taken outright, bitten through.
How bizarre, how devastating,
yet commonplace, fate can be.

Consumption

See, hear...act

There are no women in Taliban Afghanistan
(none that we can see).
There are no bigots in America
(none that we can hear),
(with my media switched off, ok).
There is Free speech in Putin's Russia
(but none that we can hear).

There are casualties of war
(while soldier rapists reap their reward)
witness raw fleshy stumps and reliance on crutches,
(No landmines seen).
There are few child abuse victims to be believed,
(they"re too young or too intimidated to speak).

There are no animals liable to extinction,
(animals don"t speak or are already gone).
Violence is remembered by many,
even if not openly spoken of in the home,
(entrenched broken spirits and intimidation are telling).

Industrial toxins don't escape,
(innocents die without justifiable cause).
There is a lack of goodwill among us,
(about which we need to act before we next speak,
good faith dictates).

consumption

1. The hearth of the matter,
how slow it burns
when left untended,
lying low, flickering,
a residue of flame
feeding upon self as fuel.

The hearth fire may flare
when sparked afresh,
but not, as may be fantasised,
setting faggots alight
beneath a martyr writhing,
bound at the end of life
to a burning stake,
no less disconcerting
for being death for true belief.

2. Within us there may be an inferno,
suppressed, that flares on occasion
then resettles to the same slow combustion,
contained as before.

We live for not yet
having been suffocated by smoke,
although part-choked
when stabbing at and stoking
coals of shame and blame.
At times we are scorched by sparks
spat out from a grate,
inflaming suppressed pain again.

3. Will the hearth's lingering consumption
of each small matter, each paltry piece,
each stick, branch, shred or twig,
limb or bark or green tops,
matter that is matted or knotted,
thrust up from roots beneath,
bring us some end, reduction or relief,
bring us some light, as well as heat,
to our brown and dried-up grief?

Ablaze!

Aflame!
Since then I have fired away,
blazed like the sun
and not yet burnt.
I've hot-handed that which I touched,
fanned rage with my heated speech,
seared the flammable within my reach,
and trod hot foot in a blistering rush
to spread flame.

Even in my quiescent days
I sparked when stoked at my hearth,
my coals radiating tolerable heat,
and on occasion bursting alight,
me aspiring to be a bonfire
on the Guy's celebration night.

And so to my dried-up days,
fuelled by diminishing brushwood.
A measure of my burn today
may be what remains to fire tomorrow.

Oh, see...

1. *Oh, see the boys of summer,*
glistening in these their golden days,
beneath a cherished sun,
setting no store beyond its heat.

Oh, see the girls of summer too,
glowing in the same lazy haze,
waving, not frowning,
busting to shine: Shine! Girls! Shine!

But these basking, bronzed wild-life,
creatures of honed self-adoration,
do not scratch beyond their immediate itch.

These boys and girls of summer daze
are curdlers in their ways,
they give the finger to the future
and, for now, it seems they can and will.

2. *Oh, see their children, their flesh replicated,*
although they do not yet exist, they will come,
thrashing their tails toward an opening, some day,
spawn yearning to feel and respond to the sun.

3. Oh, see the boys and girls of summer
now facing their winter ruin,
captive amid their own corralled waste,
wishing to be freed and on the move again,
but moving less assuredly than in their youth.

Browned skins, once merely tanned,
become dried and weathered,
creased and cracked by the sun.
Where was their assurance
that the sun's blazing furnace
would not bake their exposed flesh?

These ageing, doleful boys and girls
of post-midsummer blight,
now face miserable, inclement weathers,
any pulse of warmth immobilised in ice.

4. Oh, see the boys and girls of summer,
driftwood, sheltering, reflecting
upon those their golden days…

Big Top Emotion

1. Under the big circus top of emotion
powerful creatures connive,
(tigers, lions, bulls, bears).
Unbounded when their strength is unleashed,
they strive to break their cage constraints.
Muscled with animal empowerment,
they pace and fret in narrow confinement
(baboons, hyenas, wolves)
restrained for now,
full feelings held back from show,
watchful each moment, ready to spring.

2. Their fervour unleashed,
freed of confinement,
these beasts rage into the ring
overpowering bystanders,
(clowns, acrobats, fire-breathers)
ready to devour those who cower,
especially the unbrave and the stupid,
(turkeys, wombats, galahs)
who may be in their way,
none spared assault for want of cause,
*(recalling nightmares, apparitions,
demons and hellhounds).*

There are people who,
shot full of emotion,
like circus cannons
are ready to let fly.

Too Big

Watch your blindspot,
my true indication is uncertain.

1. Wedged to fit within
the confines of my car,
I'm sat in the driver's seat,
which barely accommodates
my weight and spread.
I strain for speed
even if feeling motion sick.

A pedestrian pace
is not my style.
Gift me a roomy hatchback,
an elongated coupe,
a decadent limousine
with a cheesy grille,
that's more my marque.

My car doesn't go fast.
I am unable to accept
less than best,
when i splutter down motorways
with diminished drive and spark.

My sweaty hands slip
on my non-slip steering wheel.
My expansive body is restless,
I have to rearrange myself,
don't look.

2. Headlights beaming
in dense daylight,
my bladder is burning,
where's the nearest piss stop?
My shock absorbers don't spare me
the road's rough ride.

3. My head rubs
against my car's roof,
that's all the headroom
I'm able to max,
my elbow is angled
out my window
like a flightless wing.
I'm trapped in my compact.

My handbrake slipped off,
I accelerate downslope,
airbags ready, I hope,
speedometer surging.
I'm spurting sweat
like petrol from a leaky pump.
My emissions, when outed,
evidence my self-pollution.

4. The road ahead is too twisty
for me to steer its tight chicanes.
I need a bigger, better car.
I'm too tall and broad
for this mini-space.
I'm stuck in my habitual gear,
my odometer crawling,
my horn is set to honk,
beep, beep, beep, beep,
bonk.

I once carried a passenger,
but i was misunderstood.
She exited upon taking exception
to being sat in my back seat.
I thought that's where
she would want to be
for greater comfort,
not parked against me.
But it seems, again,
I was thinking of myself.
In her eyes I was selfish,
it was the wrong thing
to do by her.

5. What's wrong with my car?
Viral transmission? Sunken chassis?
Suspension erratic?
Traction weak? Driver fatigue?

But even if I am indiscrete
in making my complaint,
should I accept my discomfort,
this misfit?...
I am too big for my car...

it's little niggling things

Little things,
niggling, tiny things,
may bring you down.
They come around, linger, spread, surround.
They may come to seem to be acquaintance,
familiars over time, not always sussed,
seeming not of great import,
not much recorded or analysed.

They may get you in the end
because as a matter of course,
even though not welcomed,
they are tolerated, they persist,
you reap penalties for their neglect.

It will be a lasting struggle,
with you evading them.
Little things breed best when left alone
to spread here, there and elsewhere.
So, little things continue to pervade,
seemingly immune from defeat,
until you aren't aroused any longer,
saying you are not too troubled by them
when you most recently meet.

Notice Me

the kiss

Buried in our kiss,
our bodies dance about our lips,
we thrust and fuse,
breast to breast, hip to hip.

Our lips present again.
You're drawn to me
and descend into my mouth
and throat, catching my breath.

You're the gasp of giddying smoke
swirling about my senses,
warming my blood,
lightening my head,
mulling my mood.

I'm a tar baby, I'm drawing
on Mother's nicotine tit.
The mouthing sensation,
the alkaloid hit,
drawn down, I'm content.

Unhand craving's grip, you say?
Douse the spark that fires me, abstain?
It's easier to stub out
stale talk of refrain
and clutch another light.

Reigniting my passion, I'm gratified.
And before the release
of more intertwining smoke,
there is a warm peace inside me.
Breathing out,
I follow its dissipation,
smoke curls playing in the air,
before my eyes and yours,
like our enduring embrace.

smoking desire on Psych Ward 2B

*Like watching the wind
that I can never see,
I'm hearing a voice
that keeps talking at me.*

1. Drawing on another cigarette,
after stubbing out my latest butt,
screwing up another emptied pack,
finally shuffling toward inside
from out the fenced-off back garden.
Yes, what a drag it is,
this and every lingering day.

2. Puff was a magic dragon,
his weed cast an entrancing spell.
I lit up in anticipation,
drew back, to satisfaction
behind a smoke screen.

3. The sunless smokers' lounge
and the garden's confining bounds
are near the sum total of my daily space,
where I pace, grappling with my rant,
for want of no other
to whom I can speak.

4. I'm a matchstick man,
my phosphorus head
set upon wooden stock,
a striking habit,
ingrained in my brain,
a payback legacy from my smoking days.
(How words may play
and strain to disguise
smoke blown my way.)

5. I'm sifting through rubbish,
my eyes are scouring floors
for something more.
For something tossed,
something lost,
someone else's foil.
On a good day I'm unwrapping
someone's misplaced hoard,
a lucky finder's spoil.

6. Now, from lungs
to throat to mouth,
for lack of breath, I barrk,
hack up and spit out,
not yet my dying deposit
but something else,
– old lang slime.

Not long now,
not long to go,
(but still too long,
a flickering flame
torments me still).

Notice me *(Assurance)*

1. Anyone
can be a nobody,
but I'm not, not me.
Notice me now.
I'm right here.
Turn your eyes
and ears my way.
Have regard to me.
Drink me in.

Notice me.
I am young.
I have the eyes,
the nose, the smile,
the sweep of hair,
the body profile.
I measure up,
right size.
I have the clothes
and shoes and swank
to swan down any walk,
to make the talk,
to cut the style.

Notice me.
Speak to me and listen.
Reach, tap into me. Feel,
touch, hold, shelter me.
I won't be left alone
in the cold.

2. *(Assurance.)*
I'm chic, chichi,
I'm worth the having.
I'm giving (if I'm given)
and not given to waiting.
So notice me, choose me,
give me a ring, call.

Anybody
can be a no one,
a nothing at all.
Without a following
I will founder,
I will sink for sure
into dark withdrawal.
What I need is 'bright focus'.

Notice me, notice me,
I'm here for having,
waving for the attention
I'm craving.
Choose me, choose me,
help fix my life.

your dying, your memory

1. Sudden death being so bizarre,
I listened intently as the teller told.
No quick, sure-fire assessment made.
Too distracted by my thoughts
tumbling about inside my head,
as the words were said.
The revelation, its immediacy,
unwelcome, reality brutally exposed,
a young life broken
upon her fall from the footbridge
onto the highway below.

You are gone.
You are revealed to be
someone known to me,
but not well understood.
Someone I may see sometimes,
occasionally we speak,
nothing of note, now this.

2. At your funeral, I sensed
something of your former
flowering existence
in the white roses in bloom
on top of your box,
your body, within,
to be disposed.

I stabbed my thumb on a thorn
as I picked up a white rose.
Blood oozing, staunched,
not healing quickly thereafter.
The stab was deep.

3. The first year past
since you fell from us,
I thought back to your untimely funeral,
the unnatural intimacy
of your private tragedy exposed,
and the white rose
that I bent down to pick up.
I thought,
'Once you were a spotless white rose'
while you shed your petals in your box.

Again, in my mind, you leap from the footbridge,
committing yourself to the road below.
I can't fathom your self-destruction.

Why jump?
There are those you leave
badly affected in your aftermath.
Who benefits by your premature exit?

Upon your death's anniversary
some say that
some small things
pushed you to despair.
We should know better
than to speculate.

I expect a reprise
of my thumb's throb,
pulsing on,
but none is felt.

really & imaginable

Maybe it is not a rose.
Maybe nothing such exists,
even when brushed
lovingly with lips.

1. Everyday, barely challenged,
delusion strong arms
and wrestles with me,
promoting its heresies,
reshaping my thought as to
what I should hear and see.

Unknowable stars cluster in my sky
emerge, grow and merge,
spreading out to an imagined cosmos,
one studded with stellar apparitions,
impressing
my alterable states of mind.

2. What kind of universe
do you construct?
One that is kind to you
or one that just kinda happens
to grow to any shape or form?

Make your own universe, as I do,
steadily building, building and arranging
cosmic detritus at hand.
You're in command it seems,
your inchoate creation not governed
by laws of real physics,
rather by the state of your states of mind.

Such construction is a god-like diversion
until, upon a big bang, a beach bully
kicks your sandman in the nuts,
reducing your work
to flattened, formless grains,
scattered beyond your reach,
but just as many
and seeming as real as before.

Imacello

1. At your invitation I recline my head and relax.
I'm flanked each side by the insides of your thighs.
I wait to accommodate your inclination.

I'm in your hands, from my curled scroll
down to the endpin upon which I pivot,
assured by your unwavering grip,
pleasured by your hand
lightly fingering at my box
as you please.

2. I'm a cello, moved by the sweep
and stroke of your bow
that draws me to vent this lay,
to amplify our harmonic.

Now, you grip me firmly
by my nape and draw your long bow
over the bridge across the strings
that vibrate my wooden heart.
It swells and will burst.

3. Although limited in range,
in your hands I am sonorous and deep,
resonating to your pitch throughout our exchange.

Your flesh and I sway
to the movement of your rod.
I am the driven servant of your mastery.
You pluck my strings and pause,
and muse upon the thought
that I am captive to your cause.

4. I am your device
and at your direction
I am a sounding board of a passion
that is yours and mine.
Silent, I'm the same,
wood and wire as before.
I'm a cello, play me.

footsteps, dance floor

Life demands attention to your footwork
whether you feel the need to heed or not.
Feet feed rhythm to keep in step
with the beat upon the dance floor.

1. Pop music relays to our ears
and we swagger about
to the throb of some juvenile beat.
Later, to mid-life melodies,
we shuffle off from centre stage.

While waltzing in embrace,
wrapped up in our delusion,
an apparent golden slipper fate,
this seems too good to last.
We chop and change steps
we do not change our tempo.
While dancing to time,
time is outpacing us,
our movement is falling
behind the tick o'clock.

2. I, a once would be prancer,
who could shimmy and jive,
do not do so now, having cold feet.
Our pas de deux is not to finale
with a pas de douce.

The choreography we step to is
a prelude to the danse macabre.
At times we are in and out of sync,
we tread on each others' toes,
we try to lead and not follow,
and together we stumble
toward a common brink.

I've nothing more to say,
not having the inclination
to repeat any often-spoken wisdoms.
I should've said it all before.
For you and me, the end is come,
footsteps, dance floor, no more.

About the Author

Peter Knight lives in the world's second most isolated major city, Perth, Western Australia, on the fringe of a continental desert and the sparsely populated eastern shore of the Indian Ocean.

He worked as a lawyer, mostly as an employee of the Australian Securities & Investment Commission for 25 years. Prior to that he worked as a clerk for government legal entities including the Family Court & the Perth Court of Petty Sessions. Before that he worked in unskilled jobs and as a trainee psychiatric nurse in now defunct mental asylums in Sydney & New Norfolk, Tasmania. That experience influenced how he perceives the range of the human condition.

In his early 20's he lived in other Australian cities & in Greater Manchester, UK, where his wife Audrey grew up. In relative isolation he developed his own selection and treatment of the subject matters of his poems, tending to a philosophic or surrealist approach and avoiding intellectual pretension.

www.ingramcontent.com/pod-product-compliance
Lightning Source LLC
Chambersburg PA
CBHW071914070526
44583CB00016B/1978